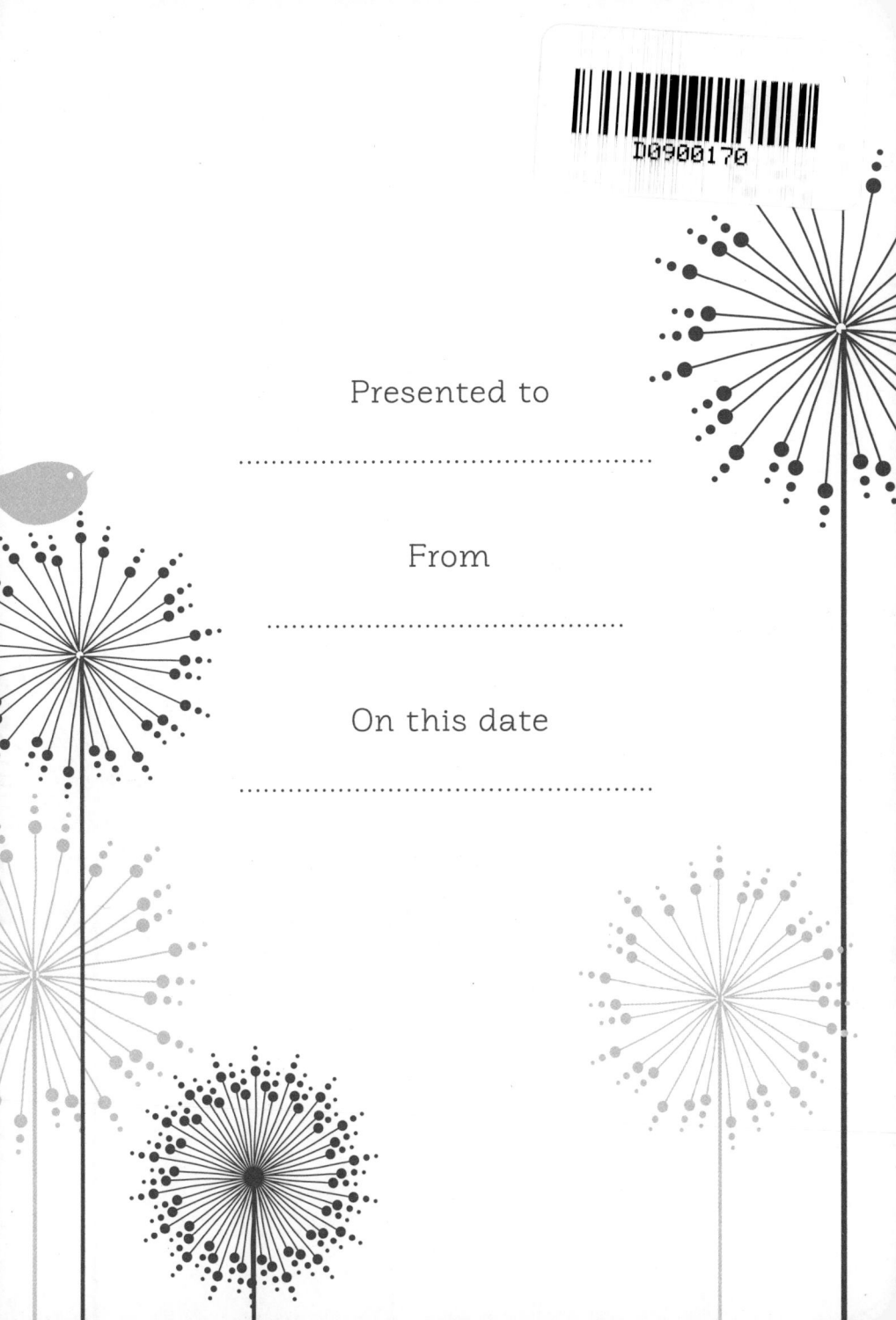

Presented to

....

From

....

On this date

....

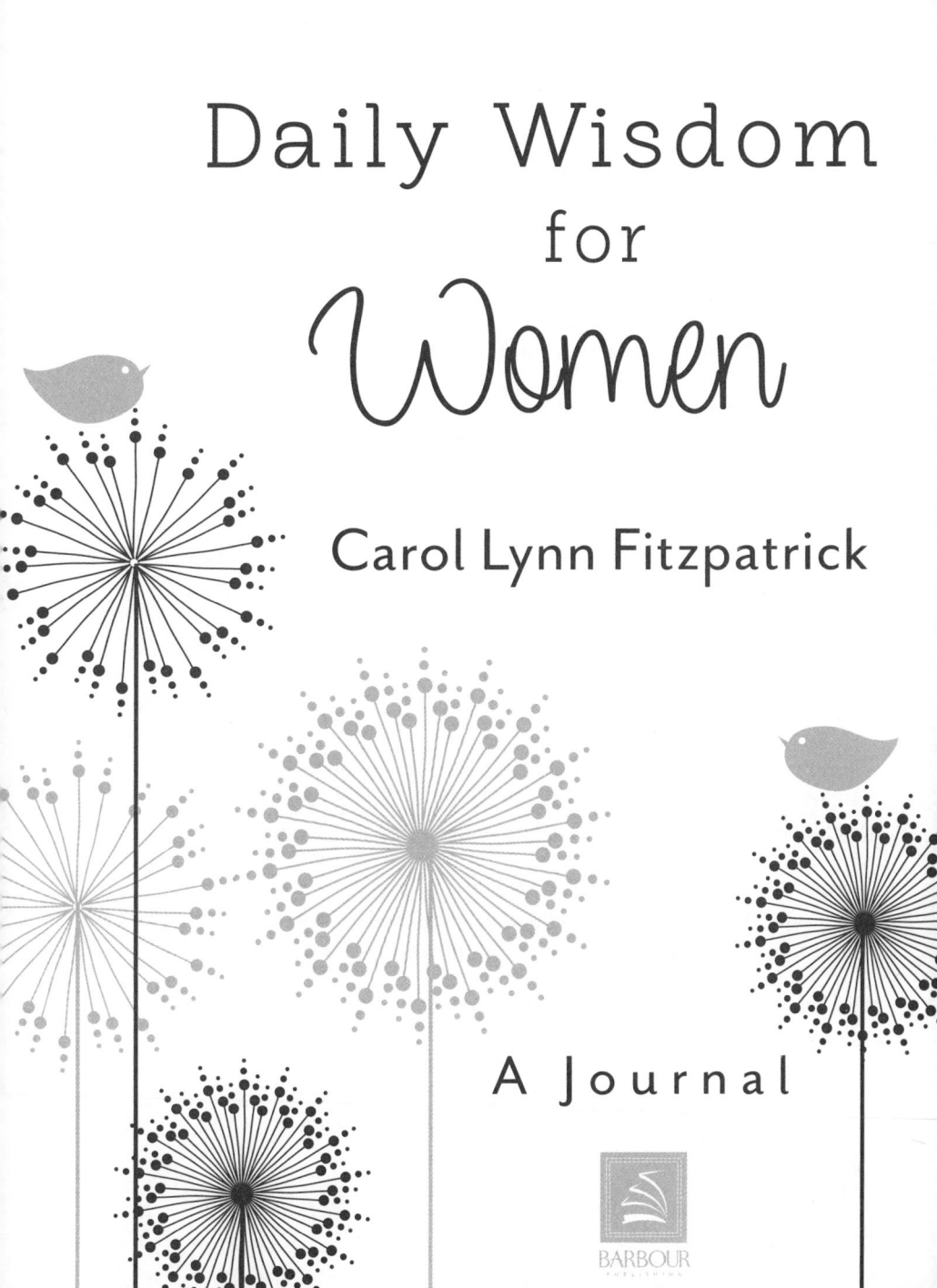

Daily Wisdom
for
Women

Carol Lynn Fitzpatrick

A Journal

BARBOUR

Print ISBN 978-1-62836-655-6

eBook Editions:
Adobe Digital Edition (.epub) 978-1-63058-116-9
Kindle and MobiPocket Edition (.prc) 978-1-63058-117-6

Published by Barbour Publishing, Inc., P.O. Box 719, Uhrichsville, Ohio 44683, www.barbourbooks.com

Our mission is to publish and distribute inspirational products offering exceptional value and biblical encouragement to the masses.

 Member of the
Evangelical Christian
Publishers Association

Printed in China.

Introduction

You are a woman of God.
You were created by Him. . .
You were blessed by Him. . .

Experience an intimate connection to your
heavenly Father with this inspiring journal.
Featuring devotional thoughts, prayers, and
scripture selections from the bestselling *Daily
Wisdom for Women*, this beautiful volume provides
encouragement and comfort for your soul. Enhance
your spiritual journey with the refreshing readings—
and come to know just how deeply and tenderly
God loves you.

Every day God freely displays His blessings. Are we too busy or disinterested to appreciate their wonder? Even if we've forgotten He's there, reminders are all around for He is the God of covenants. In a world where promises (or covenants) are disregarded routinely, I need God's kind of stability.

Lord, only You can renew my weary
spirit and fill me with fresh expectation.
Keep my eyes on Your rainbows!

....

....

....

....

....

....

....

....

....

....

....

....

....

....

....

....

....
....
....
....
....
....
....
....
....
....
....
....
....
....
....
....
....
....
....
....

I have set my rainbow in the clouds, and it will be the sign of the covenant between me and the earth. . . . Whenever the rainbow appears in the clouds, I will see it and rememberw the everlasting covenant between God and all living creatures of every kind on the earth.
GENESIS 9:13, 16 NIV

Jesus came not only to save but to teach men and women how to have a true servant's heart. The substance of ministry is service. When the apostles agreed to follow Christ, they accepted the call on His terms, not theirs.

Lord, show me clearly where I can be of
service within my local body of believers.
Perhaps there's a small hand in the
Sunday school just waiting to be held.

"Come, follow me," Jesus said,
"and I will send you out to fish for people."
MATTHEW 4:19 NIV

Gaius provided genuine hospitality, and evidently this included opening his own home, heart, and pocketbook to others, that the Word of God might go forth.

If only we all might have such pure motives for assisting others, that they might receive God's Word and see His love flowing all around them. Such a practical ministry of serving God gives honor to God, is a penetrating witness to the lost, and is a way of demonstrating obedience to God.

The elder to the beloved Gaius, whom I love in truth...
Beloved, you are acting faithfully in whatever you accomplish
for the brethren, and especially when they are strangers; and they
have testified to your love before the church. You will do well to
send them on their way in a manner worthy of God.
3 JOHN 1:1, 5–6

As we come before the Lord we first need to honor Him as Creator, Master, Savior, and Lord. Reflect on who He is, and praise Him. And because we're human, we need to confess and repent of our daily sins. Following this we should be in a mode of thanksgiving. Finally, our prayer requests should be upheld. My usual order for requests is self, family members, and life's pressing issues.

Your prayers certainly don't have to be elaborate or polished. God does not judge your way with words. He knows your heart. He wants to hear from you.

"And when you are praying, do not use meaningless repetition as the Gentiles do, for they suppose that they will be heard for their many words."
MATTHEW 6:7

God's Word says wisdom is truly a gift since it comes from the mouth of God, from the very words He speaks. And all God's Words have been written down for us, through the inspiration of the Holy Spirit. Know that if you hold fast to the precepts contained in the Bible, you will walk in integrity. Instead of gravitating toward potholes, your feet will be planted on the straight and narrow road.

....

....

....

....

....

....

....

....

....

....

....

....

....

....

....

....

....

....

....

*For the LORD gives wisdom; from His mouth come knowledge
and understanding. He stores up sound wisdom for the upright;
He is a shield to those who walk in integrity, guarding the paths
of justice, and He preserves the way of His godly ones.*
PROVERBS 2:6–8

God gave us a way to recognize the true teachers from the "wolves." "You will know them by their fruits," Scripture says. Those who abide in Christ preach the message that is consistent with the one Christ Himself taught. That salvation comes to us by the grace of God and is obtained through the belief that Christ's blood, shed on Calvary's cross, has cleansed us from our sin.

Lord, there are so many voices. Please help us to hear Yours, so that we won't be led astray by the wolves in sheep's clothing.

....

....

....

....

....

....

....

....

....

....

....

....

....

....

....

....

"Beware of the false prophets, who come to you in sheep's clothing, but inwardly are ravenous wolves. You will know them by their fruits. Grapes are not gathered from thorn bushes nor figs from thistles, are they?"
MATTHEW 7:15–16

When I first read Matthew 8:23–25, the Lord reminded me of some previous difficulties I'd encountered. The disciples were in the midst of a storm, just as I had been. Yet Jesus was with them in the boat. They woke Him, in the throes of panic, sure that the waves would swallow them up. Many times in the past I succumbed to this same degree of pandemonium. The storms of life will attempt to ravage me, but Christ is there. He will carry me safely to the other side of the shore.

When He got into the boat, His disciples followed Him. And behold,
there arose a great storm on the sea, so that the boat was being covered
with the waves; but Jesus Himself was asleep. And they came to
Him and woke Him, saying, "Save us, Lord; we are perishing!"
MATTHEW 8:23–25

Satan, whose dominion is the world, has devoted all his efforts to eradicating Christianity. Yet, though the evil one's influence can seem as ugly as an ink stain, Satan's mark on this earth will not be permanent. The reason? God's Son, Jesus Christ, lives forever within those who call upon His name. And despite the efforts of the evil one, Jesus will remain King and will one day soon come back to claim this earth for His own, forever and ever.

....
....
....
....
....
....
....
....
....
....
....
....
....
....
....
....
....
....
....
....
....

The LORD is King forever and ever;
nations have perished from His land.
PSALM 10:16

"Why do bad things happen to good people?" Our life on earth is one big test. And contrary to those who like to promote the idea of reincarnation or past life regression, Hebrews 9:27 states emphatically that we all get just one go-round, and after we die comes judgment. Life is not only a test, it is a choice.

Lord, remind me of Your presence throughout the day.
Help me to reflect Your Son Jesus Christ.

*The Lord is in His holy temple; the Lord's throne is in heaven;
His eyes behold, His eyelids test the sons of men. The Lord tests the
righteous and the wicked, and the one who loves violence His soul
hates. Upon the wicked He will rain snares; fire and brimstone and
burning wind will be the portion of their cup. For the Lord is righteous,
He loves righteousness; the upright will behold His face.*

PSALM 11:4–7

Who are the faithful? They are the ones who continue to follow God, no matter what obstacles are thrown in their path. One of the faithful, a dear friend who has debilitating multiple sclerosis, is one of the most joyful Christians I know. Jo must be assisted to the podium, but once seated on a wooden stool the weakness in her legs is forgotten. The songs that emanate from her wondrous spirit are a radiant tribute to her Savior, Jesus Christ.

*Help, Lord, for the godly man ceases to be, for the faithful disappear
from among the sons of men. They speak falsehood to one another;
with flattering lips and with a double heart they speak.*
PSALM 12:1–2

The Israelites had no idea that a great depth of darkness had overtaken them until they were in the midst of it. God previously had provided them with great light, for He communicated directly with their leaders. But the Israelites chose to act as though the switch of truth had never been turned on. They were caught up in the dark snare of idolatry. How we spend our time is but a habit, and habits can be changed by repatterning our actions. Walk in the light, as your Father intended.

The people who walk in darkness will see a great light;
those who live in a dark land, the light will shine on them.
ISAIAH 9:2

Perhaps you remember this account from Sunday school, as it's often used to reinforce God's expectation of purity: Joseph could neither dishonor Potiphar, an Egyptian officer of the Pharaoh, nor disobey his God. God had a plan. Joseph's moral stand preserved the very ancestral line leading up to Jesus Christ.

Lord, I can't look ahead to see how a critical moment of obedience fits into Your overall plan. Please give me Your strength when my human desires threaten to overpower me.

*Now Joseph was well-built and handsome, and after
a while his master's wife took notice of Joseph and said,
"Come to bed with me!" But he refused.*
GENESIS 39:6–8 NIV

Jesus spoke to the great multitude that had followed Him to the seashore. How well He knew that just because they followed didn't mean they desired to hear His message or respond in faith. Therefore, He spoke in parables, or words of truth hidden under an imaginary net. Only with the hand of faith could these followers lift a corner of the net and view the truth. Yet to those whom He knew would respond, He provided plain words.

. . . .

. . . .

. . . .

. . . .

. . . .

. . . .

. . . .

. . . .

. . . .

. . . .

. . . .

. . . .

. . . .

. . . .

. . . .

. . . .

. . . .

. . . .

. . . .

. . . .

And the disciples came and said to Him,
"Why do You speak to them in parables?"
MATTHEW 13:10

Jesus encountered narrow-minded pessimists, those who claimed they knew Him from way back. Ridiculing Him, they said, "Isn't He just a carpenter's son?" Yes, He surely was, but that carpenter was the Master Builder! For Jesus wasn't Joseph's son, but God's Son.

He came from God, full of wisdom. Those who stood with Him during His earthly ministry had true wisdom and understanding from God. Today, you obtain wisdom through a personal knowledge of Christ and by studying His Word. For only then can God's Spirit fill you with the wisdom you'll need to find and live out your God-given purpose.

. . . .

. . . .

. . . .

. . . .

. . . .

. . . .

. . . .

. . . .

. . . .

. . . .

. . . .

. . . .

. . . .

. . . .

. . . .

. . . .

. . . .

. . . .

. . . .

*He came to His hometown and began teaching them in their
synagogue, so that they were astonished, and said, "Where
did this man get this wisdom and these miraculous powers?"*
MATTHEW 13:54

Have you ever known desperation? A time when even the ground beneath you seemed unable to support you? Perhaps you were exactly where God wanted you, and yet untold trials and tribulations were heaped on you anyway. Did you doubt God's presence? Did you realize that He could act in your behalf, despite the obvious circumstances?

The very nature and character of God demands that He rescue those whom He loves. When confronted with a crisis, you can put your life in His hands.

....
....
....
....
....
....
....
....
....
....
....
....
....
....
....
....
....

....
....
....
....
....
....
....
....
....
....
....
....
....
....
....
....
....
....
....
....
....

*He reached down from on high and took hold of me; he drew
me out of deep waters. He rescued me from my powerful enemy,
from my foes, who were too strong for me. They confronted me
in the day of my disaster, but the LORD was my support.*
PSALM 18:16–18 NIV

The same "I Am" who spoke to Jacob's forefathers is also speaking to him in Genesis 46. Next, the Lord confirms the Abrahamic covenant to Jacob. For although Jacob and his family go into Egypt as a remnant of only seventy, they will become "a great nation." God promises to be with Jacob there, giving him the assurance that he's not only in God's will but that God's presence will accompany him to this new homeland.

The promises of the future will be filled with futility if God has not claimed His rightful place in your home.

....
....
....
....
....
....
....
....
....
....
....
....
....
....
....
....
....

_"I am God, the God of your father," he said. "Do not be afraid to go
down to Egypt, for I will make you into a great nation there. I will go
down to Egypt with you, and I will surely bring you back again.
And Joseph's own hand will close your eyes."_
GENESIS 46:3–4 NIV

How many of us could forgive as Joseph did? His jealous siblings had kidnapped him, thrown him into a pit, and then allowed him to be sold into slavery. Yet Joseph trusted that from God's perspective, not his own, his trials had a purpose.

Lord, sometimes I want to enjoy my agony awhile longer.
Show me the brilliance of Your forgiveness that I might trust
You in the trial and not miss the outcome You've planned.

....

....

....

....

....

....

....

....

....

....

....

....

....

....

....

....

....

....

....

....

Then Joseph said to his brothers, "Please come closer to me." And they came closer. And he said, "I am your brother Joseph, whom you sold into Egypt. Now do not be grieved or angry with yourselves, because you sold me here, for God sent me before you to preserve life."
GENESIS 45:4–5

Jesus used a physical reality to get across a spiritual truth. But the people missed the point. His warning concerned the teachings of their religious leaders, men who knew the Scriptures and yet denied Jesus as the Messiah. Although the people marveled, saying, "No one has ever made a man born blind see," they failed to have enough faith to realize that Jesus Christ was in fact "God with them."

What miracle has Jesus accomplished in your life? And yet do you see with the eyes of faith who He really is?

....

....

....

....

....

....

....

....

....

....

....

....

....

....

....

....

....

....

. . . .

. . . .

. . . .

. . . .

. . . .

. . . .

. . . .

. . . .

. . . .

. . . .

. . . .

. . . .

. . . .

. . . .

. . . .

. . . .

. . . .

. . . .

. . . .

. . . .

*"How is it that you do not understand that I did not speak
to you concerning bread? But beware of the leaven
of the Pharisees and Sadducees."*
MATTHEW 16:11

God revealed His plan to Moses, a plan to bring the Israelites out of Egypt. When Moses asks God, "Who am I that I should go to Pharaoh and bring the Israelites out of Egypt?", it comes from the heart of one who has murdered and knows his guilt before God. But instead of rebuke, Moses hears, "I will be with you. . . . I AM WHO I AM" (Exodus 3:11–12, 14 NIV). This is the same "I Am" who calls you to serve Him today.

....

....

....

....

....

....

....

....

....

....

....

....

....

....

....

....

....

....

....

*The man said, "Who made you ruler and judge over us? Are you
thinking of killing me as you killed the Egyptian?" Then Moses
was afraid and thought, "What I did must have become known."*
EXODUS 2:14 NIV

"Who do you say I am?" Jesus repeatedly asked this question to those who followed after Him. He knew that in a short while He would be gone from the face of the earth and all that these fledgling Christians would have to bolster their faith were His words and actions. Jesus wanted to be sure they understood.

Lord, if I have allowed the world's viewpoint to diminish who You are, let me now see the truth. Let me declare as Peter did, "You are the Messiah, the Son of the living God."

"But what about you?" he asked. "Who do you say I am?" Simon Peter answered, "You are the Messiah, the Son of the living God."
MATTHEW 16:15–16 NIV

Jesus, separated from the Father because of our sin, reached the ear of God with His own desperation. He experienced for us this ultimate terror...that we would never be forsaken or walk alone on the road that leads to Calvary.

Lord, no matter what hazards are down the road, You've got a signpost ready to hang on whatever misleading marker is already in the ground. And the Son is shining ahead!

....

....

....

....

....

....

....

....

....

....

....

....

....

....

....

....

....

....

....

....

....

....

My God, my God, why have You forsaken me? Far from
my deliverance are the words of my groaning.
PSALM 22:1

Poor Moses. . . God didn't appoint him spokesperson for the Israelites to watch him fail. So what was the problem? Moses heard God's voice clearly calling him to this position. Why was he balking at the task?

Moses needed to understand that God's power is limitless. Instead, Moses settled for allowing Aaron to speak for him.

Do you give the Lord part of your problem and then halfway through start solving it yourself?

....

....

....

....

....

....

....

....

....

....

....

....

....

....

....

....

. . . .

. . . .

. . . .

. . . .

. . . .

. . . .

. . . .

. . . .

. . . .

. . . .

. . . .

. . . .

. . . .

. . . .

. . . .

. . . .

. . . .

. . . .

. . . .

. . . .

. . . .

Then Moses said to the LORD, "Please, Lord, I have never been eloquent, neither recently nor in time past, nor since You have spoken to Your servant; for I am slow of speech and slow of tongue."
EXODUS 4:10

One would think that with an admission like we find in Exodus 9:27, especially from an unbelieving ruler, the man had finally seen the light. Pharaoh sounds ready to commit his heart and soul to the almighty God. Wrong! Although the Egyptians had already suffered through seven plagues, brought on by Pharaoh's stubborn refusal to allow the Israelites to leave, Pharaoh still wasn't really convinced of God's power.

Lord, it's so easy to see Pharaoh's obstinate streak.
Give me strength to admit when I'm wrong.
Give me strength to come to You in repentance.

....

....

....

....

....

....

....

....

....

....

....

....

....

....

*Then Pharaoh sent for Moses and Aaron, and said to them,
"I have sinned this time; the L*ORD* is the righteous one,
and I and my people are the wicked ones."*
EXODUS 9:27

Peter, always so practical, basically said to Jesus (in Matthew 19): "Lord, when we get to the end, will it have been worth it to follow You?" And Jesus reassures him with a gigantic yes!

None of us will just occupy space in heaven. Our God is always productive. And this job to which Jesus refers, that of judging the twelve tribes of Israel, will be given to the disciples.

Lord, I can't even imagine what You have in store for me in heaven. Please keep me faithful to complete the duties You've called me to on earth.

Then Peter said to Him, "Behold, we have left everything and followed You; what then will there be for us?" And Jesus said to them, "Truly I say to you, that you who have followed Me, in the regeneration when the Son of Man will sit on His glorious throne, you also shall sit upon twelve thrones, judging the twelve tribes of Israel."
MATTHEW 19:27–28

In old movies facial tics, winking and darting eyes, handlebar mustaches, or too much makeup helped us identify crooks and scoundrels. In real life they're not so easy to recognize. We're well aware of body language today. By simply analyzing a person's posture we can anticipate our competition's next move. But true scoundrels devise other methods of subterfuge. Whom can we trust? The Ancient of Days, who always remains the same. He alone continues to guide and direct our paths.

A troublemaker and a villain, who goes about with a corrupt mouth, who winks maliciously with his eye, signals with his feet and motions with his fingers, who plots evil with deceit in his heart—he always stirs up conflict.
PROVERBS 6:12–14 NIV

Finally the Israelites were on their way. They had lived in Egypt for 430 years. Can we even fathom the logistical nightmare of moving millions of people? And don't forget, they took the sheep, all the livestock, and even the silver, gold, and clothing they managed to wrangle from the Egyptians.

Now talk about fanfare! As they leave, their mighty God positions Himself before them, leading them in a pillar of cloud.

Lord, let me not forget that I have seen Your power.
Help me to continue walking in obedience to You.

....

....

....

....

....

....

....

....

....

....

....

....

....

....

....

....

....

....

....

....

....

*Then they set out from Succoth and camped in Etham on the edge
of the wilderness. The Lord was going before them in a pillar of cloud
by day to lead them on the way, and in a pillar of fire by night to
give them light, that they might travel by day and by night.*
EXODUS 13:20–21

When God sent His Son to earth, He invited all men and women to a wedding feast. Those who accept the invitation become part of the Church. And the Church is the bride of Christ. But there are many who have offered feeble excuses for their lack of faith.

The Son is the Bridegroom for whom the wedding feast is prepared. God Himself has laid the groundwork in the hearts that will respond to His Son, Jesus Christ.

Lord, You've invited me to dine with You.
Let me graciously accept my "wedding clothes."

....

....

....

....

....

....

....

....

....

....

....

....

....

....

....

....

....

....

....

....

....

....

*"The kingdom of heaven may be compared to a king who gave a
wedding feast for his son. And he sent out his slaves to call those who
had been invited to the wedding feast, and they were unwilling to come."*
MATTHEW 22:2–3

The demands of this world, and the pace at which our technology is racing, can sometimes overwhelm us, causing feelings of panic, powerlessness, and even paranoia. Is there a solution that brings life back into perspective? Yes. And God calls it prayer.

Spirit of God, fall afresh on me that I might lift my voice in petition to You.

....

....

....

....

....

....

....

....

....

....

....

....

....

....

....

....

....

....

*First of all, then, I urge that entreaties and prayers, petitions
and thanksgivings, be made on behalf of all men, for kings and
all who are in authority, so that we may lead a tranquil and
quiet life in all godliness and dignity. This is good and acceptable
in the sight of God our Savior, who desires all men to be saved
and to come to the knowledge of the truth.*

1 TIMOTHY 2:1–4

As mothers, grandmothers, stepmothers, and aunts, we have a God-ordained call to teach children the Word of God that they might someday enter the kingdom of God. Jesus said: "Whoever causes one of these little ones who believe in Me to stumble, it would be better for him to have a heavy millstone hung around his neck, and to be drowned in the depth of the sea" (Matthew 18:6).

That's pretty strong language. But look at the stakes! A child's whole life can be altered by someone who turns them away from the truth of Jesus Christ.

···

···

···

···

···

···

···

···

···

···

···

···

···

···

···

···

···

···

*Therefore, putting aside all malice and all deceit and hypocrisy
and envy and all slander, like newborn babies, long for the pure
milk of the word, so that by it you may grow in respect to salvation,
if you have tasted the kindness of the Lord.*

1 PETER 2:1–3

As Christians we are called to encourage one another in the faith. Paul, who spent so much of his own life in prison, had a deep understanding of the need for the reassurance and hope that the Lord richly supplied. This reliance on God's abundant source of blessings overflowed from his heart, spilling out to his fellow Christians.

Do nothing from selfishness or empty conceit, but with humility of mind regard one another as more important than yourselves; do not merely look out for your own personal interests, but also for the interests of others.
PHILIPPIANS 2:3-4

Notice that the priests were appointed by God to minister directly to Him. God didn't want them to forget whom they served.

The original priestly vestments had a significant purpose. The ephod, with the breastpiece attached, symbolized seeking wisdom or judgment from God. It was fastened on each shoulder by two onyx clasps that had the names of six tribes engraved on each clasp.

As you come before the Lord today, whatever you're wearing and wherever you are, reflect on these Old Testament times.

Thank You, Jesus, for teaching us simply to talk to You.

"These are the garments which they shall make: a breastpiece and an ephod. . .and they shall make holy garments for Aaron your brother and his sons, that he may minister as priest to Me."
EXODUS 28:4

Peter was convinced that his faith in Christ was so strong nothing could cause it to crumble. Yet only a few hours later he cowered when a young servant girl accused him of being one of Jesus' followers. And then he openly denied his Lord. Later that night, Peter would know without any doubt that Jesus had tried to warn him. Then he would look into those intense eyes and understand that because Christ went to Calvary even this sin of denial could be forgiven.

....

....

....

....

....

....

....

....

....

....

....

....

....

....

....

....

....

....

....

Then Jesus said to them, "You will all fall away because of Me this night, for it is written, 'I WILL STRIKE DOWN THE SHEPHERD, AND THE SHEEP OF THE FLOCK SHALL BE SCATTERED.' But after I have been raised, I will go ahead of you to Galilee." But Peter said to Him, "Even though all may fall away because of You, I will never fall away."
MATTHEW 26:31–33

What existed before anything else? God. And now woman and man come along, filling in a narrow blip of time, and state that all of creation "just simply evolved." Get a clue! God designed, planned, and implemented all that we do see and everything we can't comprehend. Somehow we have turned around history. Humans are not in charge. God is. And He's still commanding the dawn to happen and the earth to keep spinning and the stars to remain in the sky. Aren't you glad?

....

....

....

....

....

....

....

....

....

....

....

....

....

....

....

....

....

....

*"The LORD possessed me at the beginning of His way, before His
works of old. From everlasting I was established, from the beginning,
from the earliest times of the earth. When there were no depths I was
brought forth, when there were no springs abounding with water. . .
When He marked out the foundations of the earth; then I
was beside Him, as a master workman."*
PROVERBS 8:22–24, 29–30

When was the last time your whole community agreed on anything? Imagine everyone's talents, skills, and resources united for a common purpose!

As those in Moses' day brought all they possessed, we can surrender our own time and talents. A dear "saint" at my own church writes notes of encouragement to all who request prayer. How blessed we are to receive her "wisdom from the Lord" when we're depleted by life's challenges.

How is God using you in His Church?

....

....

....

....

....

....

....

....

....

....

....

....

....

....

....

....

....

Then the whole Israelite community withdrew from Moses' presence, and everyone who was willing and whose heart moved them came and brought an offering to the LORD for the work on the tent of meeting, for all its service, and for the sacred garments.
EXODUS 35:20-21 NIV

Years ago the popular movie *Love Story* coined the unforgettable phrase, "Love means never having to say you're sorry." What a fallacy, and more is the pity for those who bought into this lie! For love demands that we always say we're sorry. How else can relationships be restored?

Is there someone from whom you are estranged who is waiting to hear those two little words? Say you're sorry.

. . . .

. . . .

. . . .

. . . .

. . . .

. . . .

. . . .

. . . .

. . . .

. . . .

. . . .

. . . .

. . . .

. . . .

. . . .

. . . .

. . . .

They spat on Him, and took the reed and began to beat Him on the head. After they had mocked Him, they took the scarlet robe off Him and put His own garments back on Him, and led Him away to crucify Him.

MATTHEW 27:30–31

God communicated His Word and His desire for proper worship through His chosen leaders. These spokesmen then communicated His message to His chosen people. Before the coming of the Holy Spirit, at Pentecost, this chain of command was vital so that God's flock was not misled.

God required proper and orderly worship. Only an unblemished male animal could be used as the burnt offering. Down through the ages men and women were to make a connection between this sacrifice and the one Christ would willingly make on Calvary's cross.

....

....

....

....

....

....

....

....

....

....

....

....

....

....

....

....

....

....

....

....

"Speak to the sons of Israel and say to them, 'When any man of you brings an offering to the LORD, you shall bring your offering of animals from the herd or the flock.'"
LEVITICUS 1:1–2

Notice that the disciples told Jesus "immediately" of the older woman's ailment. It was time for the Sabbath meal, and Peter's wife was probably tending to the needs of her mother rather than making dinner. As soon as they arrived in the home, the disciples told Jesus about this problem. It's a high-priority, crisis-magnitude predicament! Dinner is not ready!

Jesus tenderly takes the woman's hand and instantly heals her. None of this "weakness after a fever" stuff. The dear old saint gets up and prepares the meal!

Jesus meets every need for every situation if we come to Him in faith.

....

....

....

....

....

....

....

....

....

....

....

....

....

....

....

Now Simon's mother-in-law was lying sick with a fever;
and immediately they spoke to Jesus about her. And He
came to her and raised her up, taking her by the hand,
and the fever left her, and she waited on them.
MARK 1:30–31

Mary and Christ's half brothers, James and Jude, had come looking for Him. Everywhere Jesus went such a crowd gathered around for healing that He and the disciples couldn't eat a meal in peace. His mother was worried out of love. From the perspective of His siblings, Christ's ministry had become more important than sustenance. They were saying, "He has lost His senses" (Mark 3:21).

Do we stand alongside those in our families who dare to make a difference? Or have we added to their burdens by missing their obvious purpose?

A crowd was sitting around Him, and they said to Him, "Behold, Your mother and Your brothers are outside looking for You." Answering them, He said, "Who are My mother and My brothers?.... For whoever does the will of God, he is My brother and sister and mother."
MARK 3:32–33, 35

After reading her story in Mark 5, the wonder is that this dear woman could survive for twelve long years. For that phrase, "endured much," means she "suffered something or experienced evil." She'd become a challenge to physicians of that day.

In one last-ditch effort she reaches out to touch the garment of Jesus as He passes by. She doesn't bother to call out to Him or even ask for help. Somehow she knows that His very holiness can heal her physically.

Lord, You heal me when I come to You by renewing my spirit and deepening my faith. I worship Your majesty and power.

....

....

....

....

....

....

....

....

....

....

....

....

....

....

....

....

....

....

....

A woman who had had a hemorrhage for twelve years, and had endured much at the hands of many physicians, and had spent all that she had and was not helped at all, but rather had grown worse—after hearing about Jesus, she came up in the crowd behind Him and touched His cloak. For she thought, "If I just touch His garments, I will get well."
MARK 5:25-28

Ever gone on a diet? As soon as you start one, the compulsion to eat things you never desired before becomes an overpowering beast! We know that the right foods are good for us, but we can't block out the joyfully intoxicating flavors of the ones that are off-limits.

In the days prior to refrigeration and pasteurization, if the Israelites hadn't obeyed God's dietary laws most if not all of them would have died from bacterial infections, food poisoning, and so on. God was preserving a nation from which the Messiah would be born.

....

....

....

....

....

....

....

....

....

....

....

....

....

....

....

....

....

....

....

*"Speak to the sons of Israel, saying, 'These are the creatures
which you may eat from all the animals that are on the earth.
Whatever divides a hoof, thus making split hoofs, and chews
the cud, among the animals, that you may eat.'"*
LEVITICUS 11:2-3

Hurrying toward the hospital nursery, the nurse cradled a soft pink blanket against her starched white uniform. "Wait," cried a dark-haired man in his forties. "I think that's our baby!" he shouted excitedly. As he viewed a petite head full of dark curls, all doubt was removed. "Just look at this perfect parcel," murmured the nurse in response, obviously accustomed to greeting glowing relatives.

God rejoiced at your birth. You were fashioned exactly the way He wanted you. How incredible to comprehend that when you awake in the morning, God is already thinking about you!

*For You formed my inward parts; You wove me in my mother's
womb. I will give thanks to You, for I am fearfully and wonderfully
made; wonderful are Your works, and my soul knows it very well.
My frame was not hidden from You, when I was made in secret,
and skillfully wrought in the depths of the earth.*
PSALM 139:13–15

From the rich and famous to the poor and hopeless, inestimable numbers of women and men consult astrologers before making major decisions. As Christians we know that no human possesses the ability to access knowledge of future events. The attribute of omniscience, being all-knowing, belongs to God alone.

God wants us to trust Him for our future. To know our life span would affect us every day of our life. So, God has guarded this secret as a great favor to us.

"Lord, make me to know my end and what is the extent of my days; let me know how transient I am. Behold, You have made my days as handbreadths, and my lifetime as nothing in Your sight; surely every man at his best is a mere breath."
Psalm 39:4–5

The only true "superhero" is Jesus Christ, who will never fail us. He alone was fully God and fully man. Therefore, He alone possesses perfectly all the characteristics we most admire. For He remains faithful, just, loving, omnipotent, and eternal.

Peter, an apostle of Jesus Christ, to those who reside as aliens. . .who are chosen according to the foreknowledge of God the Father, by the sanctifying work of the Spirit, to obey Jesus Christ and be sprinkled with His blood: May grace and peace be yours in the fullest measure.
1 PETER 1:1–2

A Gentile woman of Syrophoenician heritage sought out Jesus. A desperate woman, she recognized that her little daughter was demon possessed. She not only displayed faith in His ability to heal, but she believed she had the right to ask Him for assistance.

Jesus came to bring the Good News to the Jews first. But this woman, a Gentile, says she needs Jesus' touch, too. And He responds to her faith. Ask Jesus to touch your life this day.

Jesus left that place and went to the vicinity of Tyre.
He entered a house and did not want anyone to know it;
yet he could not keep his presence secret. In fact, as soon
as she heard about him, a woman whose little daughter was
possessed by an impure spirit came and fell at his feet.
MARK 7:24–25 NIV

When God gave the laws to Moses, writing them with His own hand upon the tablets of stone, He expected them to be observed. From His perspective they were commandments, not "suggestions."

But how could sinful men ever comply consistently with these laws? Therefore, throughout Old Testament history humanity was to look forward in time and trust God for the coming Messiah.

Our hope lies in the fact that Jesus Christ has paid the penalty for all our sins, on Calvary's cross. And if we confess our sins to Him, then He is faithful and just to forgive us.

....
....
....
....
....
....
....
....
....
....
....
....
....
....
....
....
....
....
....
....

" 'You shall consecrate yourselves therefore and be holy, for I am
the LORD your God. You shall keep My statutes and practice them;
I am the LORD who sanctifies you. . . . You are therefore to keep all
My statutes and all My ordinances and do them, so that the land
to which I am bringing you to live will not spew you out.' "
LEVITICUS 20:7–8, 22

The Greek word for the phenomenon of transfiguration is *metamorphoo*, from which we derive our word *metamorphosis*. Christ performs the miracle of metamorphosis in us when we come to believe in Him as Lord and Savior. He transforms us, quickening our spirits, so that we are destined to spend eternity with God in heaven. It's a change on the inside that is displayed on the outside—for the unbelieving world to see.

*Jesus took with Him Peter and James and John.... And He was
transfigured before them; and His garments became radiant and
exceedingly white, as no launderer on earth can whiten them. Elijah
appeared to them along with Moses; and they were talking with Jesus.*
MARK 9:2–4

"Faith comes from hearing, and hearing by the word of Christ" (Romans 10:17). This kind of dynamic faith involves the whole person. If someone professes their belief in God and yet does not take the Word to others, and does not attend a weekly Bible study, and can't be bothered to help those in obvious need, it makes me wonder whether that faith is real. For there has to be some outward manifestation of the change that takes place inwardly.

．．

．．

．．

．．

．．

You believe that God is one. You do well; the demons also believe, and shudder. But are you willing to recognize, you foolish fellow, that faith without works is useless? Was not Abraham our father justified by works when he offered up Isaac his son on the altar? You see that faith was working with his works, and as a result of the works, faith was perfected; and the Scripture was fulfilled which says, "AND ABRAHAM BELIEVED GOD, AND IT WAS RECKONED TO HIM AS RIGHTEOUSNESS," and he was called the friend of God.

JAMES 2:19–23

When God created the world, He not only planned your place in it, but He also reserved a place in heaven for you. Now, you can either claim your ticket by accepting Christ's salvation on your behalf, or you can cancel the reservation by never responding to God's offer.

Remember Paul's encounter with that blinding light? He knew when Christ appeared to him that God had intervened to change the very course of his life: "Paul, an apostle of Christ Jesus by the will of God. . ." (2 Corinthians 1:1). God extended to Paul the truth about Jesus Christ, and he responded in commitment.

Blessed be the God and Father of our Lord Jesus Christ, who has blessed us with every spiritual blessing in the heavenly places in Christ, just as He chose us in Him before the foundation of the world, that we would be holy and blameless before Him.
EPHESIANS 1:3–4

One of the mental exercises college students wrestle with in basic psychology courses concerns unanswerable questions. For example, "What would you say is your least desirable personality trait?" Now, who is going to answer this without trying to put a positive spin on it?

This is the kind of squeeze play the Pharisees and scribes tried constantly to force Jesus into. No matter what Jesus said, He'd be wrong. And yet this tactic always backfired on them.

Jesus Christ cannot be fooled. He knew the hearts of the Pharisees and scribes, and He knows your heart, too.

*The chief priests and the scribes and the elders came to Him, and
began saying to Him, "By what authority are You doing these things, or
who gave You this authority to do these things?" And Jesus said to them,
"I will ask you one question, and you answer Me, and then I will tell
you by what authority I do these things. Was the baptism of
John from heaven, or from men? Answer Me."*
MARK 11:27–30

Christ explained to the Pharisees that the reason they couldn't comprehend what would take place in the Resurrection was because they understood neither the Scriptures nor the power of God (Mark 12:24).

All of us are responsible not only to read the Word of God with understanding but also to have discernment concerning the clergy who minister to us. Is their primary goal to make sure their flock is ultimately led to God's glory?

And Jesus began to say, as He taught in the temple, "How is it that the scribes say that the Christ is the son of David? David himself said in the Holy Spirit, 'THE LORD SAID TO MY LORD, "SIT AT MY RIGHT HAND, UNTIL I PUT YOUR ENEMIES BENEATH YOUR FEET."' David himself calls Him 'Lord'; so in what sense is He his son?"
MARK 12:35-37

Instead of being a cause of terror in our hearts, that phrase, "fear of the Lord" means to reverence and honor Him as God. For He alone is God, righteous, and wise enough to intervene and effect positive changes in our lives. Instilling this truth in our children enables them to know the ways of the Lord.

Obedience always brings inner peace, contentment, and happiness, while stepping out from underneath God's umbrella of protection only gets us soaked and saturated with sin.

*The fear of the L*ORD *prolongs life, but the years of the wicked will be shortened. The hope of the righteous is gladness, but the expectation of the wicked perishes. The way of the L*ORD *is a stronghold to the upright, but ruin to the workers of iniquity. The righteous will never be shaken, but the wicked will not dwell in the land.*
PROVERBS 10:27–30

Do you ever wake up thinking about someone you may not have seen in years? Well, that's a "God call." God may be prompting your heart to respond to that person's need for encouragement.

The writer of the Book of Hebrews spoke with conviction and understanding. "Encourage one another day after day, as long as it is still called 'Today,' so that none of you will be hardened by the deceitfulness of sin. For we have become partakers of Christ, if we hold fast the beginning of our assurance firm until the end" (Hebrews 3:13–14).

Therefore, holy brethren, partakers of a heavenly calling, consider Jesus, the Apostle and High Priest of our confession; He was faithful to Him who appointed Him, as Moses also was in all His house. For He has been counted worthy of more glory than Moses, by just so much as the builder of the house has more honor than the house. For every house is built by someone, but the builder of all things is God.
HEBREWS 3:1–4

Like a good parent, God left Miriam to mull over her rebellious and questioning spirit for seven days. And then the Lord graciously healed her, at the request of Moses.

How could she even think of asking God to explain Himself? But don't we all do the same thing when the going gets rough? How about, "If there's a God, then why is there so much suffering?" Well, guess what? Men and women are harming one another. God is not responsible for our sinful nature.

"Not so, with My servant Moses, he is faithful in all My household; with him I speak mouth to mouth, even openly, and not in dark sayings, and he beholds the form of the Lord. Why then were you not afraid to speak against My servant, against Moses?"
Numbers 12:7–8

Korah didn't want to be called a sinner. Surely he must have known that only God knew the true condition of man's depravity. Yet he opted to pretend this fight for control existed between him and Moses instead of between him and God.

Do you fight for control of your life? Surrender the ultimate control to God and realize the freedom of His perfect plan.

Lord, please open my eyes to my own sin,
and prevent me from leading others astray.

....
....
....
....
....
....
....
....
....
....
....
....
....
....
....
....
....
....
....
....
....

Now Korah the son of Izhar, the son of Kohath, the son of Levi, with Dathan and Abiram, the sons of Eliab, and On the son of Peleth, sons of Reuben, took action, and they rose up before Moses, together with some of the sons of Israel, two hundred and fifty leaders of the congregation.
NUMBERS 16:1–2

Mark 15:43, along with parallel passages from the other three Gospels, discloses that Joseph of Arimathea had become a secret disciple of Christ. Yet now, accompanied by Nicodemus, another member of the ruling council of religious leaders, Joseph of Arimathea displayed an incredible boldness of character. For Joseph requested Christ's body for burial, then he and Nicodemus lovingly prepared their Lord for His burial.

Lord, the tomb is empty, and the grave clothes left behind signify for all time that You have risen from the dead. And because You live, we can face whatever tomorrow brings!

Joseph of Arimathea came, a prominent member of the Council,
who himself was waiting for the kingdom of God; and he gathered up
courage and went in before Pilate, and asked for the body of Jesus.
MARK 15:43

"Love is patient, love is kind and is not jealous; love does not brag and is not arrogant, does not act unbecomingly; it does not seek its own, is not provoked, does not take into account a wrong suffered, does not rejoice in unrighteousness, but rejoices with the truth; bears all things, believes all things, hopes all things, endures all things. Love never fails" (1 Corinthians 13:4–8).

Why don't more people tap into this resource? To truly love someone means that we will always place that person's welfare above our own. This, after all, is how God loves us.

· ·

....

....

....

....

....

....

....

....

....

....

....

....

....

....

....

....

....

....

....

....

....

....

....

....

....

....

....

....

....

....

....

....

....

....

....

....

....

....

....

*If I speak with the tongues of men and of angels, but do not
have love, I have become a noisy gong or a clanging cymbal.*
1 CORINTHIANS 13:1

What the world would have lost if Zacharias had become bitter over his circumstances! He and Elizabeth were now old, and their dream of sons and daughters had become but a vapor.

One day, as he offered incense before the altar, an angel of the Lord appeared and said, "Do not be afraid, Zacharias, for your petition has been heard, and your wife Elizabeth will bear you a son, and you will give him the name John" (Luke 1:13).

Lord, restore my hope in You today.

*In the days of Herod, king of Judea, there was a priest named
Zacharias, of the division of Abijah; and he had a wife from the
daughters of Aaron, and her name was Elizabeth. They were
both righteous in the sight of God, walking blamelessly in all the
commandments and requirements of the Lord. But they had no child,
because Elizabeth was barren, and they were both advanced in years.*
LUKE 1:5–7

Anna had faithfully served in the temple her entire life. And despite her advanced age, she remained there even after others had gone home for the evening. She was a prophetess; she foretold the truths of God to the people. No wonder He used her life.

God had promised Anna that she would see the Messiah before she died. She waited eighty-four years, biding her time in service to the Lord. And He kept His word. Let us strive to follow Anna's prayerful example, and we, too, will be blessed by God.

*And there was a prophetess, Anna the daughter of Phanuel,
of the tribe of Asher. . . She never left the temple, serving night and day
with fastings and prayers. At that very moment she came up
and began giving thanks to God, and continued to speak of Him
to all those who were looking for the redemption of Jerusalem.*
LUKE 2:36–38

Counting on their heritage as a means of automatic salvation, the religious leaders called themselves Abraham's children. Yet to be Abraham's children required that they display faith.

John's exhortations were aimed at the wilderness of men's souls. How many churchgoers do you know who claim the faith yet exist in a wasteland of sin?

Lord, You sent John to proclaim Your beloved Son.
Help me to proclaim Your Word and love to anyone, anywhere.

. . . .

. . . .

. . . .

. . . .

. . . .

. . . .

. . . .

. . . .

. . . .

. . . .

. . . .

. . . .

. . . .

. . . .

. . . .

. . . .

. . . .

. . . .

. . . .

. . . .

*The word of God came to John, the son of Zacharias, in the wilderness.
And he came into all the district around the Jordan, preaching a
baptism of repentance for the forgiveness of sins; as it is written in the
book of the words of Isaiah the prophet, "THE VOICE OF ONE CRYING IN THE
WILDERNESS, 'MAKE READY THE WAY OF THE LORD, MAKE HIS PATHS STRAIGHT.'"*

LUKE 3:2-4

King David composed Psalm 61 as a song, acknowledging God as his rock. He clung with tenacity to the fact that no matter how desperate his situation appeared, God is as immovable as a boulder. Although David's trials may differ from yours, you, too, can use strong coping mechanisms.

First, David acknowledged that God remained all-powerful, despite life circumstances. And second, David looked back at God's past rescues.

Lord, I search for a way through the torrents of despair.
How precious is the knowledge that You hear and care.

Hear my cry, O God; give heed to my prayer. From the end of the earth I call to You when my heart is faint; lead me to the rock that is higher than I. For You have been a refuge for me, a tower of strength against the enemy. Let me dwell in Your tent forever; let me take refuge in the shelter of Your wings.

PSALM 61:1–4

$\mathcal{Mary}$ $\mathcal{and}$ Joseph married because they loved each other, but more importantly, both of them loved God and desired to be a part of His purpose for man. And within this environment of submission, Israel's inheritance, the Savior, remained secure.

Lord, we know that Joseph loved Mary and both were chosen by You. Yet they also obeyed You in their choice of a life partner.

· ·

· ·

· ·

· ·

· ·

· ·

· ·

· ·

· ·

· ·

· ·

· ·

· ·

· ·

· ·

· ·

· ·

· ·

"Every daughter who comes into possession of an inheritance of any tribe of the sons of Israel shall be wife to one of the family of the tribe of her father, so that the sons of Israel each may possess the inheritance of his fathers. Thus no inheritance shall be transferred from one tribe to another tribe, for the tribes of the sons of Israel shall each hold to his own inheritance."
NUMBERS 36:8–9

Have you ever found yourself so tempted to sin that you ached all the way to your soul? Christ understands that pull toward evil.

Satan wasn't just present in the wilderness to "bug" the Lord Jesus Christ. This was a full-on frontal attack. And the stakes were high. For if Christ had succumbed to Satan's snare, He would have been ineligible to make that perfect sacrifice on the cross as the Lamb of God without blemish.

Lord, I thank You for Your Son's perfect victory over Satan.

And the devil said to Him, "If You are the Son of God,
tell this stone to become bread." And Jesus answered him,
"It is written, 'MAN SHALL NOT LIVE ON BREAD ALONE.' "
LUKE 4:3-4

When pondering Jesus as the Friend of Sinners, the Lion of the Tribe of Judah, or the Alpha and Omega, your mind focuses on Him, and daily problems diminish.

David knew even in his day that taking time to praise His awesome God provided strength and renewal for his weary soul. Joyfully he worshiped!

Lord, my grateful heart declares Your Name in a world that has all but forgotten You still care.

Shout joyfully to God, all the earth; sing the
glory of His name; make His praise glorious.
PSALM 66:1–2

How can we stop ourselves from falling into sin? By remembering: "No temptation has overtaken you but such as is common to man; and God is faithful, who will not allow you to be tempted beyond what you are able, but with the temptation will provide the way of escape also, so that you will be able to endure it" (1 Corinthians 10:13).

....

....

....

....

....

....

....

....

....

....

....

....

....

....

....

....

....

....

....

....

....

....

....

....

....

....

....

....

....

....

....

....

For I do not want you to be unaware, brethren, that our fathers were all under the cloud and all passed through the sea; and all were baptized into Moses in the cloud and in the sea; and all ate the same spiritual food; and all drank the same spiritual drink, for they were drinking from a spiritual rock which followed them; and the rock was Christ. Nevertheless, with most of them God was not well-pleased; for they were laid low in the wilderness. Now these things happened as examples for us, so that we would not crave evil things as they also craved. . . . Nor let us act immorally, as some of them did, and twenty-three thousand fell in one day.

1 CORINTHIANS 10:1–6, 8

The Israelites were two million strong when they left Egypt, and now in "the fortieth year, on the first day of the eleventh month" (Deuteronomy 1:3), Moses proclaimed to them what the Lord had commanded.

Now that their wandering days were over, Moses charged these twelve tribal officials to judge fairly the disputes among the people. They were about to take possession of the land God had promised them.

Dear heavenly Father, let my trust in You never waver.
Give me wisdom and courage for this day.

*" 'The LORD your God has multiplied you, and behold, you are this day
like the stars of heaven in number. May the LORD, the God of your fathers,
increase you a thousand-fold more than you are and bless you, just as
He has promised you!... Choose wise and discerning and experienced
men from your tribes, and I will appoint them as your heads.' "*
DEUTERONOMY 1:10–11, 13

Christ prayed all night for the men who would preach, teach, heal the sick, raise the dead, and record His words. Christ chose a solitary spot, minimizing His distractions.

When it's time to do battle we need to be alone first. Then, after we know God's will, we can solicit the prayers and fellowship of others.

Lord, thank You for letting me come to You with all my burdens, large and small. Only You can give true and lasting peace.

He spent the whole night in prayer to God. And when day came,
He called His disciples to Him and chose twelve of them, whom He
also named as apostles: Simon, whom He also named Peter,
and Andrew his brother; and James and John; and Philip and
Bartholomew; and Matthew and Thomas; James the son of
Alphaeus, and Simon who was called the Zealot; Judas the son
of James, and Judas Iscariot, who became a traitor.
LUKE 6:12–16

Can't you just see poor Jonah? No human hand can pluck him from the depths as the seaweed wraps around his body and begins to suck him down into the cold, dark mire.

There in the belly of the fish, Jonah finally stopped running. Jonah eventually pledges allegiance to his God. "But I will sacrifice to You with the voice of thanksgiving. That which I have vowed I will pay. Salvation is from the LORD" (Jonah 2:9). Jonah's ears were finally ready to listen to God.

....

....

....

....

....

....

....

....

....

....

....

....

....

....

....

....

....

....

....

....

....

....

....

....

....

....

....

....

....

....

....

....

"I called out of my distress to the LORD, and He answered me. I cried for help from the depth of Sheol; You heard my voice. For You had cast me into the deep. . . . All Your breakers and billows passed over me. So I said, 'I have been expelled from Your sight. Nevertheless I will look again toward Your holy temple.' Water encompassed me to the point of death. . . . Weeds were wrapped around my head. . . . The earth with its bars was around me forever, but You have brought up my life from the pit, O LORD my God. While I was fainting away, I remembered the LORD, and my prayer came to You, into Your holy temple."

JONAH 2:2–7

The apostles were the men Christ had trained, empowered, and prepared to bring the Gospel message first to the Jews and then the Gentiles. They had been with Christ on a daily basis, learning from His example how to reach out with compassion to those in need. But instead they displayed both selfishness and a lack of love. How could they be left in charge of disseminating the Gospel? And yet they were God's Plan A.

Lord, how grateful I am that Your Holy Spirit worked in the lives of these apostles, molding them into strong men of faith.

And He called the twelve together, and gave them power and authority
over all the demons and to heal diseases. And He sent them out to
proclaim the kingdom of God and to perform healing. And He said to
them, "Take nothing for your journey, neither a staff, nor a bag,
nor bread, nor money; and do not even have two tunics apiece."

LUKE 9:1–3

Read Luke 10:38–40. Isn't this just how we feel when the men in our household excuse themselves from the table as soon as the first dirty dish appears? Martha, ever the perfect hostess, was left to do all the work. It didn't seem fair.

However, what Martha really desired was a release from her compulsive neatness. And that's when the Lord presented her with a process for "chilling out."

Have you taken time to get to know your Lord? Perhaps your life, like Martha's, is missing the best part.

....
....
....
....
....
....
....
....
....
....
....
....
....
....
....
....
....
....

A woman named Martha welcomed Him into her home. She had a sister called Mary, who was seated at the Lord's feet, listening to His word. But Martha was distracted with all her preparations; and she came up to Him and said, "Lord, do You not care that my sister has left me to do all the serving alone? Then tell her to help me."

LUKE 10:38–40

When one of the Pharisees asked Christ, " 'Teacher, which is the great commandment in the Law?' " He said to him, "YOU SHALL LOVE THE LORD YOUR GOD WITH ALL YOUR HEART, AND WITH ALL YOUR SOUL, AND WITH ALL YOUR MIND. . . . YOU SHALL LOVE YOUR NEIGHBOR AS YOURSELF" (Matthew 22:36–37, 39). Does your heart need a checkup?

Father, I know circumcision of my heart is wrought by Your Holy Spirit. Lord, make me willing to undergo transformation that I might truly love You, and others.

*Moreover the LORD your God will circumcise your heart
and the heart of your descendants, to love the LORD
your God with all your heart and with all your soul.*
DEUTERONOMY 30:6

Sometimes Jesus offered His perfect insight in parables. "To you it has been granted to know the mysteries of the kingdom of God, but to the rest it is in parables, so that SEEING THEY MAY NOT SEE, AND HEARING THEY MAY NOT UNDERSTAND" (Luke 8:10).

Jesus had just shared with them the parable about the sower. He knew that those whose hearts were open and receptive to Him would understand its meaning. On the other hand, those whose hearts held only antagonism and self-righteousness would not understand even if He spoke plainly.

Is your heart ready to listen to Jesus?

Listen, O my people, to my instruction; incline your ears to the words of my mouth. I will open my mouth in a parable; I will utter dark sayings of old, which we have heard and known, and our fathers have told us.
PSALM 78:1-3

God did not allow those who taunted Moses to challenge the authority of his successor. Moses, who is preparing to die, names Joshua as his successor. Right there, in the presence of all Israel, Moses admonishes Joshua to "be strong and courageous." God chose Joshua because he had faithfully served Moses throughout all their years in the wilderness.

Lord, I forget sometimes that those in leadership are chosen by You. And with responsibility comes accountability.

....

....

....

....

....

....

....

....

....

....

....

....

....

....

....

*"Be strong and courageous, for you shall go with this people
into the land which the LORD has sworn to their fathers to
give them, and you shall give it to them as an inheritance."*
DEUTERONOMY 31:7

How like the Israelites we are! God showed them the path they were to walk in. He even defined the boundaries for them. And yet time after time they leaped beyond the lines of safety and tried to live without Him.

Is it time for you to let God steer the course?

Lord Almighty, whatever I desperately need release from today, please show me that You're able to heal as long as my heart is willing.

....

....

....

....

....

....

....

....

....

....

....

....

....

....

....

....

....

....

....

....

....

....

"Jerusalem, Jerusalem, you who kill the prophets and stone those sent to you, how often I have longed to gather your children together, as a hen gathers her chicks under her wings, and you were not willing."
LUKE 13:34 NIV

Have you ever cried out to God for deliverance, recognizing that your own circumstances are a direct result of leaving the Lord out of the decision making? We've all been there at one time or another. But God's not surprised. He's not only aware of what we've done, He watched us make this awful choice and then witnessed the harm we did to ourselves and others.

We thank You that we can come to You as Lord and Messiah. You are truly a God of forgiveness.

....
....
....
....
....
....
....
....
....
....
....
....
....
....
....
....

....
....
....
....
....
....
....
....
....
....
....
....
....
....
....
....
....
....
....
....
....
....

Help us, O God of our salvation, for the glory of Your name; and deliver us and forgive our sins for Your name's sake. Why should the nations say, "Where is their God?" Let there be known among the nations in our sight, vengeance for the blood of Your servants which has been shed.

PSALM 79:9–10

How ecstatic this woman in Luke 15 was to find this missing coin she'd considered lost forever. When a young girl in Israel married she began wearing a headband containing ten silver coins. This band carried the same significance as our modern wedding rings. To lose one would have been nothing short of a catastrophe.

Jesus compared the woman's deep joy to the celebration that goes on in heaven when a sinner repents and "Son-beams" of peace finally flood into the soul. It's the feeling of "wholeness" a person hungers for all her life.

....
....
....
....
....
....
....
....
....
....
....
....
....
....
....
....
....
....

"Or what woman, if she has ten silver coins and loses one coin, does not light a lamp and sweep the house and search carefully until she finds it? When she has found it, she calls together her friends and neighbors, saying, 'Rejoice with me, for I have found the coin which I had lost!'"
LUKE 15:8–9

Joshua had gathered the people together, revealing the Lord's words. Then the people left their tents and followed the priests who carried the ark of the covenant. When they reached the banks of the Jordan the water stopped flowing. . .and the nation of Israel crossed over!

As the news spread of God's miracle, so had the level of terror. Jericho was "locked down and secured" behind its gates. But God instructed Israel's warriors to march around the city for six days. No obstacle can prevent God's plan from being realized!

"You shall, moreover, command the priests who are carrying the ark of the covenant, saying, 'When you come to the edge of the waters of the Jordan, you shall stand still in the Jordan.'"
JOSHUA 3:8

It still takes the knowledge of Jesus Christ to redeem our world. In Luke 17 Jesus admonished His disciples to "rebuke" their brothers if they've sinned. Why? Because sin is a progressive fall. And "real love" means intervening that we might get back on track.

Have you shared your love of Jesus with a neighbor? Pray today that God might open a door or window to your witness.

*"Be on your guard! If your brother sins,
rebuke him; and if he repents, forgive him."*
LUKE 17:3

King David had an eternal perspective. Israel constantly battled their enemies. How he must have longed for a lasting peace. But he had to settle for that little niche of peace he carved out for himself while pondering what heaven was like, anticipating the day he'd dwell with God. For the God of perfection created for Himself a place of eternal security.

What knowledge we have that God desires to share this incredible place with His imperfect creatures! Despite our sinful nature, God truly loves us with an eternal affection.

How lovely are Your dwelling places, O Lord of hosts!
My soul longed and even yearned for the courts of the Lord;
my heart and my flesh sing for joy to the living God.
PSALM 84:1–2

Back in New Testament times judges held court in a traveling tent. Whether cases were considered or not depended upon the plaintiffs' ability to "gain the attention of the judges' attendants." The widow in Luke 18 already had three strikes against her. First, as a woman she had no priority standing in the court. Second, as a widow she didn't have a husband to fight for her in these legal proceedings. And finally, without the funds to pay for assistance she was without hope.

Lord, You alone judge rightly. You alone will administer to the guilty the punishment they truly deserve.

....

....

....

....

....

....

....

....

....

....

....

....

....

....

....

....

....

....

....

....

....

....

"In a certain city there was a judge who did not fear God and did not respect man. There was a widow in that city, and she kept coming to him, saying, 'Give me legal protection from my opponent.'"
LUKE 18:2–3

One-Year Bible
Reading Schedule

1–Jan	Gen. 1–2	Matt. 1	Ps. 1
2–Jan	Gen. 3–4	Matt. 2	Ps. 2
3–Jan	Gen. 5–7	Matt. 3	Ps. 3
4–Jan	Gen. 8–10	Matt. 4	Ps. 4
5–Jan	Gen. 11–13	Matt. 5:1–20	Ps. 5
6–Jan	Gen. 14–16	Matt. 5:21–48	Ps. 6
7–Jan	Gen. 17–18	Matt. 6:1–18	Ps. 7
8–Jan	Gen. 19–20	Matt. 6:19–34	Ps. 8
9–Jan	Gen. 21–23	Matt. 7:1–11	Ps. 9:1–8
10–Jan	Gen. 24	Matt. 7:12–29	Ps. 9:9–20
11–Jan	Gen. 25–26	Matt. 8:1–17	Ps. 10:1–11
12–Jan	Gen. 27:1–28:9	Matt. 8:18–34	Ps. 10:12–18
13–Jan	Gen. 28:10–29:35	Matt. 9	Ps. 11
14–Jan	Gen. 30:1–31:21	Matt. 10:1–15	Ps. 12
15–Jan	Gen. 31:22–32:21	Matt. 10:16–36	Ps. 13
16–Jan	Gen. 32:22–34:31	Matt. 10:37–11:6	Ps. 14
17–Jan	Gen. 35–36	Matt. 11:7–24	Ps. 15
18–Jan	Gen. 37–38	Matt. 11:25–30	Ps. 16
19–Jan	Gen. 39–40	Matt. 12:1–29	Ps. 17
20–Jan	Gen. 41	Matt. 12:30–50	Ps. 18:1–15
21–Jan	Gen. 42–43	Matt. 13:1–9	Ps. 18:16–29
22–Jan	Gen. 44–45	Matt. 13:10–23	Ps. 18:30–50
23–Jan	Gen. 46:1–47:26	Matt. 13:24–43	Ps. 19
24–Jan	Gen. 47:27–49:28	Matt. 13:44–58	Ps. 20
25–Jan	Gen. 49:29–Exod. 1:22	Matt. 14	Ps. 21
26–Jan	Exod. 2–3	Matt. 15:1–28	Ps. 22:1–21
27–Jan	Exod. 4:1–5:21	Matt. 15:29–16:12	Ps. 22:22–31
28–Jan	Exod. 5:22–7:24	Matt. 16:13–28	Ps. 23
29–Jan	Exod. 7:25–9:35	Matt. 17:1–9	Ps. 24
30–Jan	Exod. 10–11	Matt. 17:10–27	Ps. 25
31–Jan	Exod. 12	Matt. 18:1–20	Ps. 26
1–Feb	Exod. 13–14	Matt. 18:21–35	Ps. 27
2–Feb	Exod. 15–16	Matt. 19:1–15	Ps. 28
3–Feb	Exod. 17–19	Matt. 19:16–30	Ps. 29
4–Feb	Exod. 20–21	Matt. 20:1–19	Ps. 30
5–Feb	Exod. 22–23	Matt. 20:20–34	Ps. 31:1–8
6–Feb	Exod. 24–25	Matt. 21:1–27	Ps. 31:9–18
7–Feb	Exod 26–27	Matt. 21:28–46	Ps. 31:19–24
8–Feb	Exod. 28	Matt. 22	Ps. 32
9–Feb	Exod. 29	Matt. 23:1–36	Ps. 33:1–12
10–Feb	Exod. 30–31	Matt. 23:37–24:28	Ps. 33:13–22
11–Feb	Exod. 32–33	Matt. 24:29–51	Ps. 34:1–7

12–Feb	Exod. 34:1–35:29	Matt. 25:1–13	Ps. 34:8–22
13–Feb	Exod. 35:30–37:29	Matt. 25:14–30	Ps. 35:1–8
14–Feb	Exod. 38–39	Matt. 25:31–46	Ps. 35:9–17
15–Feb	Exod. 40	Matt. 26:1–35	Ps. 35:18–28
16–Feb	Lev. 1–3	Matt. 26:36–68	Ps. 36:1–6
17–Feb	Lev. 4:1–5:13	Matt. 26:69–27:26	Ps. 36:7–12
18–Feb	Lev. 5:14 –7:21	Matt. 27:27–50	Ps. 37:1–6
19–Feb	Lev. 7:22–8:36	Matt. 27:51–66	Ps. 37:7–26
20–Feb	Lev. 9–10	Matt. 28	Ps. 37:27–40
21–Feb	Lev. 11–12	Mark 1:1–28	Ps. 38
22–Feb	Lev. 13	Mark 1:29–39	Ps. 39
23–Feb	Lev. 14	Mark 1:40–2:12	Ps. 40:1–8
24–Feb	Lev. 15	Mark 2:13–3:35	Ps. 40:9–17
25–Feb	Lev. 16–17	Mark 4:1–20	Ps. 41:1–4
26–Feb	Lev. 18–19	Mark 4:21–41	Ps. 41:5–13
27–Feb	Lev. 20	Mark 5	Ps. 42–43
28–Feb	Lev. 21–22	Mark 6:1–13	Ps. 44
1–Mar	Lev. 23–24	Mark 6:14–29	Ps. 45:1–5
2–Mar	Lev. 25	Mark 6:30–56	Ps. 45:6–12
3–Mar	Lev. 26	Mark 7	Ps. 45:13–17
4–Mar	Lev. 27	Mark 8	Ps. 46
5–Mar	Num. 1–2	Mark 9:1–13	Ps. 47
6–Mar	Num. 3	Mark 9:14–50	Ps. 48:1–8
7–Mar	Num. 4	Mark 10:1–34	Ps. 48:9–14
8–Mar	Num. 5:1–6:21	Mark 10:35–52	Ps. 49:1–9
9–Mar	Num. 6:22–7:47	Mark 11	Ps. 49:10–20
10–Mar	Num. 7:48–8:4	Mark 12:1–27	Ps. 50:1–15
11–Mar	Num. 8:5–9:23	Mark 12:28–44	Ps. 50:16–23
12–Mar	Num. 10–11	Mark 13:1–8	Ps. 51:1–9
13–Mar	Num. 12–13	Mark 13:9–37	Ps. 51:10–19
14–Mar	Num. 14	Mark 14:1–31	Ps. 52
15–Mar	Num. 15	Mark 14:32–72	Ps. 53
16–Mar	Num. 16	Mark 15:1–32	Ps. 54
17–Mar	Num. 17–18	Mark 15:33–47	Ps. 55
18–Mar	Num. 19–20	Mark 16	Ps. 56:1–7
19–Mar	Num. 21:1–22:20	Luke 1:1–25	Ps. 56:8–13
20–Mar	Num. 22:21–23:30	Luke 1:26–56	Ps. 57
21–Mar	Num. 24–25	Luke 1:57–2:20	Ps. 58
22–Mar	Num. 26:1–27:11	Luke 2:21–38	Ps. 59:1–8
23–Mar	Num. 27:12–29:11	Luke 2:39–52	Ps. 59:9–17
24–Mar	Num. 29:12–30:16	Luke 3	Ps. 60:1–5
25–Mar	Num. 31	Luke 4	Ps. 60:6–12

26–Mar	Num. 32–33	Luke 5:1–16	Ps. 61
27–Mar	Num. 34–36	Luke 5:17–32	Ps. 62:1–6
28–Mar	Deut. 1:1–2:25	Luke 5:33–6:11	Ps. 62:7–12
29–Mar	Deut. 2:26–4:14	Luke 6:12–35	Ps. 63:1–5
30–Mar	Deut. 4:15–5:22	Luke 6:36–49	Ps. 63:6–11
31–Mar	Deut. 5:23–7:26	Luke 7:1–17	Ps. 64:1–5
1–Apr	Deut. 8–9	Luke 7:18–35	Ps. 64:6–10
2–Apr	Deut. 10–11	Luke 7:36–8:3	Ps. 65:1–8
3–Apr	Deut. 12–13	Luke 8:4–21	Ps. 65:9–13
4–Apr	Deut. 14:1–16:8	Luke 8:22–39	Ps. 66:1–7
5–Apr	Deut. 16:9–18:22	Luke 8:40–56	Ps. 66:8–15
6–Apr	Deut. 19:1–21:9	Luke 9:1–22	Ps. 66:16–20
7–Apr	Deut. 21:10–23:8	Luke 9:23–42	Ps. 67
8–Apr	Deut. 23:9–25:19	Luke 9:43–62	Ps. 68:1–6
9–Apr	Deut. 26:1–28:14	Luke 10:1–20	Ps. 68:7–14
10–Apr	Deut. 28:15–68	Luke 10:21–37	Ps. 68:15–19
11–Apr	Deut. 29–30	Luke 10:38–11:23	Ps. 68:20–27
12–Apr	Deut. 31:1–32:22	Luke 11:24–36	Ps. 68:28–35
13–Apr	Deut. 32:23–33:29	Luke 11:37–54	Ps. 69:1–9
14–Apr	Deut. 34–Josh. 2	Luke 12:1–15	Ps. 69:10–17
15–Apr	Josh. 3:1–5:12	Luke 12:16–40	Ps. 69:18–28
16–Apr	Josh. 5:13–7:26	Luke 12:41–48	Ps. 69:29–36
17–Apr	Josh. 8–9	Luke 12:49–59	Ps. 70
18–Apr	Josh. 10:1–11:15	Luke 13:1–21	Ps. 71:1–6
19–Apr	Josh. 11:16–13:33	Luke 13:22–35	Ps. 71:7–16
20–Apr	Josh. 14–16	Luke 14:1–15	Ps. 71:17–21
21–Apr	Josh. 17:1–19:16	Luke 14:16–35	Ps. 71:22–24
22–Apr	Josh. 19:17–21:42	Luke 15:1–10	Ps. 72:1–11
23–Apr	Josh. 21:43–22:34	Luke 15:11–32	Ps. 72:12–20
24–Apr	Josh. 23–24	Luke 16:1–18	Ps. 73:1–9
25–Apr	Judg. 1–2	Luke 16:19–17:10	Ps. 73:10–20
26–Apr	Judg. 3–4	Luke 17:11–37	Ps. 73:21–28
27–Apr	Judg. 5:1–6:24	Luke 18:1–17	Ps. 74:1–3
28–Apr	Judg. 6:25–7:25	Luke 18:18–43	Ps. 74:4–11
29–Apr	Judg. 8:1–9:23	Luke 19:1–28	Ps. 74:12–17
30–Apr	Judg. 9:24–10:18	Luke 19:29–48	Ps. 74:18–23
1–May	Judg. 11:1–12:7	Luke 20:1–26	Ps. 75:1–7
2–May	Judg. 12:8–14:20	Luke 20:27–47	Ps. 75:8–10
3–May	Judg. 15–16	Luke 21:1–19	Ps. 76:1–7
4–May	Judg. 17–18	Luke 21:20–22:6	Ps. 76:8–12
5–May	Judg. 19:1–20:23	Luke 22:7–30	Ps. 77:1–11
6–May	Judg. 20:24–21:25	Luke 22:31–54	Ps. 77:12–20

7–May	Ruth 1–2	Luke 22:55–23:25	Ps. 78:1–4
8–May	Ruth 3–4	Luke 23:26–24:12	Ps. 78:5–8
9–May	1 Sam. 1:1–2:21	Luke 24:13–53	Ps. 78:9–16
10–May	1 Sam. 2:22–4:22	John 1:1–28	Ps. 78:17–24
11–May	1 Sam. 5–7	John 1:29–51	Ps. 78:25–33
12–May	1 Sam. 8:1–9:26	John 2	Ps. 78:34–41
13–May	1 Sam. 9:27–11:15	John 3:1–22	Ps. 78:42–55
14–May	1 Sam. 12–13	John 3:23–4:10	Ps. 78:56–66
15–May	1 Sam. 14	John 4:11–38	Ps. 78:67–72
16–May	1 Sam. 15–16	John 4:39–54	Ps. 79:1–7
17–May	1 Sam. 17	John 5:1–24	Ps. 79:8–13
18–May	1 Sam. 18–19	John 5:25–47	Ps. 80:1–7
19–May	1 Sam. 20–21	John 6:1–21	Ps. 80:8–19
20–May	1 Sam. 22–23	John 6:22–42	Ps. 81:1–10
21–May	1 Sam. 24:1–25:31	John 6:43–71	Ps. 81:11–16
22–May	1 Sam. 25:32–27:12	John 7:1–24	Ps. 82
23–May	1 Sam. 28–29	John 7:25–8:11	Ps. 83
24–May	1 Sam. 30–31	John 8:12–47	Ps. 84:1–4
25–May	2 Sam. 1–2	John 8:48–9:12	Ps. 84:5–12
26–May	2 Sam. 3–4	John 9:13–34	Ps. 85:1–7
27–May	2 Sam. 5:1–7:17	John 9:35–10:10	Ps. 85:8–13
28–May	2 Sam. 7:18–10:19	John 10:11–30	Ps. 86:1–10
29–May	2 Sam. 11:1–12:25	John 10:31–11:16	Ps. 86:11–17
30–May	2 Sam. 12:26–13:39	John 11:17–54	Ps. 87
31–May	2 Sam. 14:1–15:12	John 11:55–12:19	Ps. 88:1–9
1–Jun	2 Sam. 15:13–16:23	John 12:20–43	Ps. 88:10–18
2–Jun	2 Sam. 17:1–18:18	John 12:44–13:20	Ps. 89:1–6
3–Jun	2 Sam. 18:19–19:39	John 13:21–38	Ps. 89:7–13
4–Jun	2 Sam. 19:40–21:22	John 14:1–17	Ps. 89:14–18
5–Jun	2 Sam. 22:1–23:7	John 14:18–15:27	Ps. 89:19–29
6–Jun	2 Sam. 23:8–24:25	John 16:1–22	Ps. 89:30–37
7–Jun	1 Kings 1	John 16:23–17:5	Ps. 89:38–52
8–Jun	1 Kings 2	John 17:6–26	Ps. 90:1–12
9–Jun	1 Kings 3–4	John 18:1–27	Ps. 90:13–17
10–Jun	1 Kings 5–6	John 18:28–19:5	Ps. 91:1–10
11–Jun	1 Kings 7	John 19:6–25a	Ps. 91:11–16
12–Jun	1 Kings 8:1–53	John 19:25b–42	Ps. 92:1–9
13–Jun	1 Kings 8:54–10:13	John 20:1–18	Ps. 92:10–15
14–Jun	1 Kings 10:14–11:43	John 20:19–31	Ps. 93
15–Jun	1 Kings 12:1–13:10	John 21	Ps. 94:1–11
16–Jun	1 Kings 13:11–14:31	Acts 1:1–11	Ps. 94:12–23
17–Jun	1 Kings 15:1–16:20	Acts 1:12–26	Ps. 95

18–Jun	1 Kings 16:21–18:19	Acts 2:1–21	Ps. 96:1–8
19–Jun	1 Kings 18:20–19:21	Acts 2:22–41	Ps. 96:9–13
20–Jun	1 Kings 20	Acts 2:42–3:26	Ps. 97:1–6
21–Jun	1 Kings 21:1–22:28	Acts 4:1–22	Ps. 97:7–12
22–Jun	1 Kings 22:29–2 Kings 1:18	Acts 4:23–5:11	Ps. 98
23–Jun	2 Kings 2–3	Acts 5:12–28	Ps. 99
24–Jun	2 Kings 4	Acts 5:29–6:15	Ps. 100
25–Jun	2 Kings 5:1–6:23	Acts 7:1–16	Ps. 101
26–Jun	2 Kings 6:24–8:15	Acts 7:17–36	Ps. 102:1–7
27–Jun	2 Kings 8:16–9:37	Acts 7:37–53	Ps. 102:8–17
28–Jun	2 Kings 10–11	Acts 7:54–8:8	Ps. 102:18–28
29–Jun	2 Kings 12–13	Acts 8:9–40	Ps. 103:1–9
30–Jun	2 Kings 14–15	Acts 9:1–16	Ps. 103:10–14
1–Jul	2 Kings 16–17	Acts 9:17–31	Ps. 103:15–22
2–Jul	2 Kings 18:1–19:7	Acts 9:32–10:16	Ps. 104:1–9
3–Jul	2 Kings 19:8–20:21	Acts 10:17–33	Ps. 104:10–23
4–Jul	2 Kings 21:1–22:20	Acts 10:34–11:18	Ps. 104: 24–30
5–Jul	2 Kings 23	Acts 11:19–12:17	Ps. 104:31–35
6–Jul	2 Kings 24–25	Acts 12:18–13:13	Ps. 105:1–7
7–Jul	1 Chron. 1–2	Acts 13:14–43	Ps. 105:8–15
8–Jul	1 Chron. 3:1–5:10	Acts 13:44–14:10	Ps. 105:16–28
9–Jul	1 Chron. 5:11–6:81	Acts 14:11–28	Ps. 105:29–36
10–Jul	1 Chron. 7:1–9:9	Acts 15:1–18	Ps. 105:37–45
11–Jul	1 Chron. 9:10–11:9	Acts 15:19–41	Ps. 106:1–12
12–Jul	1 Chron. 11:10–12:40	Acts 16:1–15	Ps. 106:13–27
13–Jul	1 Chron. 13–15	Acts 16:16–40	Ps. 106:28–33
14–Jul	1 Chron. 16–17	Acts 17:1–14	Ps. 106:34–43
15–Jul	1 Chron. 18–20	Acts 17:15–34	Ps. 106:44–48
16–Jul	1 Chron. 21–22	Acts 18:1–23	Ps. 107:1–9
17–Jul	1 Chron. 23–25	Acts 18:24–19:10	Ps. 107:10–16
18–Jul	1 Chron. 26–27	Acts 19:11–22	Ps. 107:17–32
19–Jul	1 Chron. 28–29	Acts 19:23–41	Ps. 107:33–38
20–Jul	2 Chron. 1–3	Acts 20:1–16	Ps. 107:39–43
21–Jul	2 Chron. 4:1–6:11	Acts 20:17–38	Ps. 108
22–Jul	2 Chron. 6:12–7:10	Acts 21:1–14	Ps. 109:1–20
23–Jul	2 Chron. 7:11–9:28	Acts 21:15–32	Ps. 109:21–31
24–Jul	2 Chron. 9:29–12:16	Acts 21:33–22:16	Ps. 110:1–3
25–Jul	2 Chron. 13–15	Acts 22:17–23:11	Ps. 110:4–7
26–Jul	2 Chron. 16–17	Acts 23:12–24:21	Ps. 111
27–Jul	2 Chron. 18–19	Acts 24:22–25:12	Ps. 112
28–Jul	2 Chron. 20–21	Acts 25:13–27	Ps. 113
29–Jul	2 Chron. 22–23	Acts 26	Ps. 114

30–Jul	2 Chron. 24:1–25:16	Acts 27:1–20	Ps. 115:1–10
31–Jul	2 Chron. 25:17–27:9	Acts 27:21–28:6	Ps. 115:11–18
1–Aug	2 Chron. 28:1–29:19	Acts 28:7–31	Ps. 116:1–5
2–Aug	2 Chron. 29:20–30:27	Rom. 1:1–17	Ps. 116:6–19
3–Aug	2 Chron. 31–32	Rom. 1:18–32	Ps. 117
4–Aug	2 Chron. 33:1–34:7	Rom. 2	Ps. 118:1–18
5–Aug	2 Chron. 34:8–35:19	Rom. 3:1–26	Ps. 118:19–23
6–Aug	2 Chron. 35:20–36:23	Rom. 3:27–4:25	Ps. 118:24–29
7–Aug	Ezra 1–3	Rom. 5	Ps. 119:1–8
8–Aug	Ezra 4–5	Rom. 6:1–7:6	Ps. 119:9–16
9–Aug	Ezra 6:1–7:26	Rom. 7:7–25	Ps. 119:17–32
10–Aug	Ezra 7:27–9:4	Rom. 8:1–27	Ps. 119:33–40
11–Aug	Ezra 9:5–10:44	Rom. 8:28–39	Ps. 119:41–64
12–Aug	Neh. 1:1–3:16	Rom. 9:1–18	Ps. 119:65–72
13–Aug	Neh. 3:17–5:13	Rom. 9:19–33	Ps. 119:73–80
14–Aug	Neh. 5:14–7:73	Rom. 10:1–13	Ps. 119:81–88
15–Aug	Neh. 8:1–9:5	Rom. 10:14–11:24	Ps. 119:89–104
16–Aug	Neh. 9:6–10:27	Rom. 11:25–12:8	Ps. 119:105–120
17–Aug	Neh. 10:28–12:26	Rom. 12:9–13:7	Ps. 119:121–128
18–Aug	Neh. 12:27–13:31	Rom. 13:8–14:12	Ps. 119:129–136
19–Aug	Esther 1:1–2:18	Rom. 14:13–15:13	Ps. 119:137–152
20–Aug	Esther 2:19–5:14	Rom. 15:14–21	Ps. 119:153–168
21–Aug	Esther. 6–8	Rom. 15:22–33	Ps. 119:169–176
22–Aug	Esther 9–10	Rom. 16	Ps. 120–122
23–Aug	Job 1–3	1 Cor. 1:1–25	Ps. 123
24–Aug	Job 4–6	1 Cor. 1:26–2:16	Ps. 124–125
25–Aug	Job 7–9	1 Cor. 3	Ps. 126–127
26–Aug	Job 10–13	1 Cor. 4:1–13	Ps. 128–129
27–Aug	Job 14–16	1 Cor. 4:14–5:13	Ps. 130
28–Aug	Job 17–20	1 Cor. 6	Ps. 131
29–Aug	Job 21–23	1 Cor. 7:1–16	Ps. 132
30–Aug	Job 24–27	1 Cor. 7:17–40	Ps. 133–134
31–Aug	Job 28–30	1 Cor. 8	Ps. 135
1–Sep	Job 31–33	1 Cor. 9:1–18	Ps. 136:1–9
2–Sep	Job 34–36	1 Cor. 9:19–10:13	Ps. 136:10–26
3–Sep	Job 37–39	1 Cor. 10:14–11:1	Ps. 137
4–Sep	Job 40–42	1 Cor. 11:2–34	Ps. 138
5–Sep	Eccles. 1:1–3:15	1 Cor. 12:1–26	Ps. 139:1–6
6–Sep	Eccles. 3:16–6:12	1 Cor. 12:27–13:13	Ps. 139:7–18
7–Sep	Eccles. 7:1–9:12	1 Cor. 14:1–22	Ps. 139:19–24
8–Sep	Eccles. 9:13–12:14	1 Cor. 14:23–15:11	Ps. 140:1–8
9–Sep	SS 1–4	1 Cor. 15:12–34	Ps. 140:9–13

10–Sep	SS 5–8	1 Cor. 15:35–58	Ps. 141
11–Sep	Isa. 1–2	1 Cor. 16	Ps. 142
12–Sep	Isa. 3–5	2 Cor. 1:1–11	Ps. 143:1–6
13–Sep	Isa. 6–8	2 Cor. 1:12–2:4	Ps. 143:7–12
14–Sep	Isa. 9–10	2 Cor. 2:5–17	Ps. 144
15–Sep	Isa. 11–13	2 Cor. 3	Ps. 145
16–Sep	Isa. 14–16	2 Cor. 4	Ps. 146
17–Sep	Isa. 17–19	2 Cor. 5	Ps. 147:1–11
18–Sep	Isa. 20–23	2 Cor. 6	Ps. 147:12–20
19–Sep	Isa. 24:1–26:19	2 Cor. 7	Ps. 148
20–Sep	Isa. 26:20–28:29	2 Cor. 8	Ps. 149–150
21–Sep	Isa. 29–30	2 Cor. 9	Prov. 1:1–9
22–Sep	Isa. 31–33	2 Cor. 10	Prov. 1:10–22
23–Sep	Isa. 34–36	2 Cor. 11	Prov. 1:23–26
24–Sep	Isa. 37–38	2 Cor. 12:1–10	Prov. 1:27–33
25–Sep	Isa. 39–40	2 Cor. 12:11–13:14	Prov. 2:1–15
26–Sep	Isa. 41–42	Gal. 1	Prov. 2:16–22
27–Sep	Isa. 43:1–44:20	Gal. 2	Prov. 3:1–12
28–Sep	Isa. 44:21–46:13	Gal. 3:1–18	Prov. 3:13–26
29–Sep	Isa. 47:1–49:13	Gal 3:19–29	Prov. 3:27–35
30–Sep	Isa. 49:14–51:23	Gal 4:1–11	Prov. 4:1–19
1–Oct	Isa. 52–54	Gal. 4:12–31	Prov. 4:20–27
2–Oct	Isa. 55–57	Gal. 5	Prov. 5:1–14
3–Oct	Isa. 58–59	Gal. 6	Prov. 5:15–23
4–Oct	Isa. 60–62	Eph. 1	Prov. 6:1–5
5–Oct	Isa. 63:1–65:16	Eph. 2	Prov. 6:6–19
6–Oct	Isa. 65:17–66:24	Eph. 3:1–4:16	Prov. 6:20–26
7–Oct	Jer. 1–2	Eph. 4:17–32	Prov. 6:27–35
8–Oct	Jer. 3:1–4:22	Eph. 5	Prov. 7:1–5
9–Oct	Jer. 4:23–5:31	Eph. 6	Prov. 7:6–27
10–Oct	Jer. 6:1–7:26	Phil. 1:1–26	Prov. 8:1–11
11–Oct	Jer. 7:26–9:16	Phil. 1:27–2:18	Prov. 8:12–21
12–Oct	Jer. 9:17–11:17	Phil 2:19–30	Prov. 8:22–36
13–Oct	Jer. 11:18–13:27	Phil. 3	Prov. 9:1–6
14–Oct	Jer. 14–15	Phil. 4	Prov. 9:7–18
15–Oct	Jer. 16–17	Col. 1:1–23	Prov. 10:1–5
16–Oct	Jer. 18:1–20:6	Col. 1:24–2:15	Prov. 10:6–14
17–Oct	Jer. 20:7–22:19	Col. 2:16–3:4	Prov. 10:15–26
18–Oct	Jer. 22:20–23:40	Col. 3:5–4:1	Prov. 10:27–32
19–Oct	Jer. 24–25	Col. 4:2–18	Prov. 11:1–11
20–Oct	Jer. 26–27	1 Thess. 1:1–2:8	Prov. 11:12–21
21–Oct	Jer. 28–29	1 Thess. 2:9–3:13	Prov. 11:22–26

22–Oct	Jer. 30:1–31:22	1 Thess. 4:1–5:11	Prov. 11:27–31
23–Oct	Jer. 31:23–32:35	1 Thess. 5:12–28	Prov. 12:1–14
24–Oct	Jer. 32:36–34:7	2 Thess. 1–2	Prov. 12:15–20
25–Oct	Jer. 34:8–36:10	2 Thess. 3	Prov. 12:21–28
26–Oct	Jer. 36:11–38:13	1 Tim. 1:1–17	Prov. 13:1–4
27–Oct	Jer. 38:14–40:6	1 Tim. 1:18–3:13	Prov. 13:5–13
28–Oct	Jer. 40:7–42:22	1 Tim. 3:14–4:10	Prov. 13:14–21
29–Oct	Jer. 43–44	1 Tim. 4:11–5:16	Prov. 13:22–25
30–Oct	Jer. 45–47	1 Tim. 5:17–6:21	Prov. 14:1–6
31–Oct	Jer. 48:1–49:6	2 Tim. 1	Prov. 14:7–22
1–Nov	Jer. 49:7–50:16	2 Tim. 2	Prov. 14:23–27
2–Nov	Jer. 50:17–51:14	2 Tim. 3	Prov. 14:28–35
3–Nov	Jer. 51:15–64	2 Tim. 4	Prov. 15:1–9
4–Nov	Jer. 52–Lam. 1	Titus 1:1–9	Prov. 15:10–17
5–Nov	Lam. 2:1–3:38	Titus 1:10–2:15	Prov. 15:18–26
6–Nov	Lam. 3:39–5:22	Titus 3	Prov. 15:27–33
7–Nov	Ezek. 1:1–3:21	Philemon 1	Prov. 16:1–9
8–Nov	Ezek. 3:22–5:17	Heb. 1:1–2:4	Prov. 16:10–21
9–Nov	Ezek. 6–7	Heb. 2:5–18	Prov. 16:22–33
10–Nov	Ezek. 8–10	Heb. 3:1–4:3	Prov. 17:1–5
11–Nov	Ezek. 11–12	Heb. 4:4–5:10	Prov. 17:6–12
12–Nov	Ezek. 13–14	Heb. 5:11–6:20	Prov. 17:13–22
13–Nov	Ezek. 15:1–16:43	Heb. 7:1–28	Prov. 17:23–28
14–Nov	Ezek. 16:44–17:24	Heb. 8:1–9:10	Prov. 18:1–7
15–Nov	Ezek. 18–19	Heb. 9:11–28	Prov. 18:8–17
16–Nov	Ezek. 20	Heb. 10:1–25	Prov. 18:18–24
17–Nov	Ezek. 21–22	Heb. 10:26–39	Prov. 19:1–8
18–Nov	Ezek. 23	Heb. 11:1–31	Prov. 19:9–14
19–Nov	Ezek. 24–26	Heb. 11:32–40	Prov. 19:15–21
20–Nov	Ezek. 27–28	Heb. 12:1–13	Prov. 19:22–29
21–Nov	Ezek. 29–30	Heb. 12:14–29	Prov. 20:1–18
22–Nov	Ezek. 31–32	Heb. 13	Prov. 20:19–24
23–Nov	Ezek. 33:1–34:10	Jas. 1	Prov. 20:25–30
24–Nov	Ezek. 34:11–36:15	Jas. 2	Prov. 21:1–8
25–Nov	Ezek. 36:16–37:28	Jas. 3	Prov. 21:9–18
26–Nov	Ezek. 38–39	Jas. 4:1–5:6	Prov. 21:19–24
27–Nov	Ezek. 40	Jas. 5:7–20	Prov. 21:25–31
28–Nov	Ezek. 41:1–43:12	1 Pet. 1:1–12	Prov. 22:1–9
29–Nov	Ezek. 43:13–44:31	1 Pet. 1:13–2:3	Prov. 22:10–23
30–Nov	Ezek. 45–46	1 Pet. 2:4–17	Prov. 22:24–29
1–Dec	Ezek. 47–48	1 Pet. 2:18–3:7	Prov. 23:1–9
2–Dec	Dan. 1:1–2:23	1 Pet. 3:8–4:19	Prov. 23:10–16

3–Dec	Dan. 2:24–3:30	1 Pet. 5	Prov. 23:17–25
4–Dec	Dan. 4	2 Pet. 1	Prov. 23:26–35
5–Dec	Dan. 5	2 Pet. 2	Prov. 24:1–18
6–Dec	Dan. 6:1–7:14	2 Pet. 3	Prov. 24:19–27
7–Dec	Dan. 7:15–8:27	1 John 1:1–2:17	Prov. 24:28–34
8–Dec	Dan. 9–10	1 John 2:18–29	Prov. 25:1–12
9–Dec	Dan. 11–12	1 John 3:1–12	Prov. 25:13–17
10–Dec	Hos. 1–3	1 John 3:13–4:16	Prov. 25:18–28
11–Dec	Hos. 4–6	1 John 4:17–5:21	Prov. 26:1–16
12–Dec	Hos. 7–10	2 John	Prov. 26:17–21
13–Dec	Hos. 11–14	3 John	Prov. 26:22–27:9
14–Dec	Joel 1:1–2:17	Jude	Prov. 27:10–17
15–Dec	Joel 2:18–3:21	Rev. 1:1–2:11	Prov. 27:18–27
16–Dec	Amos 1:1–4:5	Rev. 2:12–29	Prov. 28:1–8
17–Dec	Amos 4:6–6:14	Rev. 3	Prov. 28:9–16
18–Dec	Amos 7–9	Rev. 4:1–5:5	Prov. 28:17–24
19–Dec	Obad.–Jonah	Rev. 5:6–14	Prov. 28:25–28
20–Dec	Mic. 1:1–4:5	Rev. 6:1–7:8	Prov. 29:1–8
21–Dec	Mic. 4:6–7:20	Rev. 7:9–8:13	Prov. 29:9–14
22–Dec	Nah. 1–3	Rev. 9–10	Prov. 29:15–23
23–Dec	Hab. 1–3	Rev. 11	Prov. 29:24–27
24–Dec	Zeph. 1–3	Rev. 12	Prov. 30:1–6
25–Dec	Hag. 1–2	Rev. 13:1–14:13	Prov. 30:7–16
26–Dec	Zech. 1–4	Rev. 14:14–16:3	Prov. 30:17–20
27–Dec	Zech. 5–8	Rev. 16:4–21	Prov. 30:21–28
28–Dec	Zech. 9–11	Rev. 17:1–18:8	Prov. 30:29–33
29–Dec	Zech. 12–14	Rev. 18:9–24	Prov. 31:1–9
30–Dec	Mal. 1–2	Rev. 19–20	Prov. 31:10–17
31–Dec	Mal. 3–4	Rev. 21–22	Prov. 31:18–31

About the Author

Carol Lynn Fitzpatrick is a bestselling author of nine books that have totaled nearly three quarters of a million books sold. Her *Daily Wisdom for Women* appeared on the CBA (Christian Booksellers Association) Ten Best Sellers List for many years. Carol has been married for forty years to a now-retired military officer. They have three grown children and three grandchildren. Although she credits her Midwest upbringing for instilling her core values, she has lived in California for nearly four decades.